WHAT WAS THE DUST BOWL?

ENVIRONMENT AND SOCIETY

Children's Environment Books

Speedy Publishing LLC
40 E. Main St. #1156
Newark, DE 19711
www.speedypublishing.com

In this book, we're going to talk about the Dust Bowl. So, let's get right to it!

When we think of problems in the environment, we often think of hurricanes, tornadoes, or floods. However, too much water or wind isn't the only type of environmental problem that's severe. During the 1930s, there was a serious drought in the region of the Great Plains and it created what was later called a *"Dust Bowl."* The term *"Dust Bowl"* was used to describe both the region where it was happening as well as what was happening.

Dust Storm in Rolla, Kansas. May 6, 1935.

WHAT WAS THE DUST BOWL?

The Dust Bowl, also called the Dirty Thirties, was a period of intense storms of dust that damaged both the American as well as the Canadian prairies. In the United States, the southwestern section of Kansas, the southeast portion of Colorado and the panhandles of both Texas as well as Oklahoma were affected by this environmental disaster.

Soil blown by dust bowl winds piled up in large drifts on a Kansas farm. March 1936.

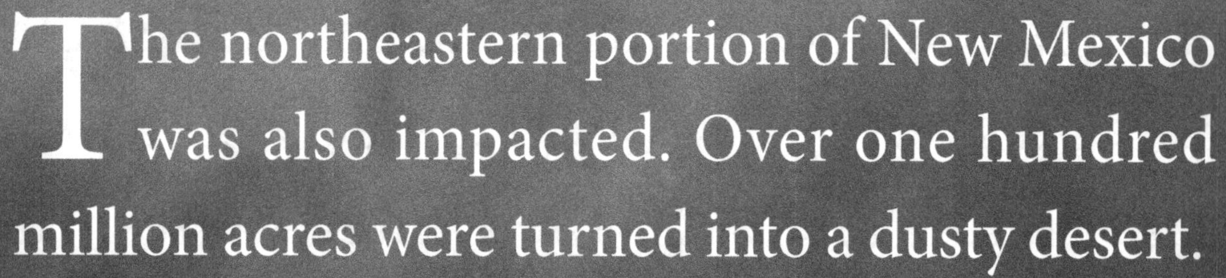

The northeastern portion of New Mexico was also impacted. Over one hundred million acres were turned into a dusty desert.

Heavy black clouds of dust rising over the Texas Panhandle, Texas. March 1936.

WHERE DID ALL THE DUST COME FROM?

The dust came from farming methods that didn't keep the soil anchored. For a ten-year period of time, farmers had continued to plow the previously untouched topsoil that covered the Great Plains. Prior to this farming, there had been native grasses with deep roots. The roots of these grasses kept the soil and moisture in place even during periods of intense, high winds and drought.

A dust storm in Hugoton Kansas 1936.

The farmers had attempted to convert these grasslands to farming soil by using gasoline tractors and combine harvesters to the land so that it could be used for farming. However, the grassland that they were trying to use, generally received only 10 inches of rain every year.

SOIL DRIFTING OVER HOG HOUSE — S. DAK. —1935

Then, the 1930s happened and there was almost no rain. The drought continued for many years. Now that the grasslands had been destroyed, the topsoil was no longer anchored and began to turn to dry dust. This disaster along with the economic horrors of the Great Depression must have made farmers feel that they were experiencing the end of the world.

Soil drifting over a farm building on a South Dakota farm in 1935.

At that time, farmers didn't know how to prevent these types of environmental problems with advanced farming techniques designed to prevent the loss of topsoil. In later decades, plows were invented that would break up and loosen the soil while still leaving more than 80% of the plant material and residue material on the top. Also, instead of leaving half a farm with just bare soil, farmers take care to only leave about one third of their farms without crops.

Dust storms near Lawrence Kansas.

A huge dust storm moves across the land during the Dust Bowl of the 1930s.

$\mathbf{A}$ third factor that contributed to improved farming practices was irrigation, which took place in the 1950s. This ensured that the soil didn't dry out as it had in the 1930s. It's safe to say that due to these methods, there will never be another full-scale Dust Bowl in the United States again.

HUGE DUST STORMS

As more and more of the soil turned to dust, enormous dust storms began to form across the Great Plains. There was so much dust in the atmosphere that people were having difficulty breathing. Houses were sometimes buried under the piles of dust. The dust storms became so massive that under certain weather conditions they traveled from the west all the way to the East Coast.

Abandoned house, Haskell, Kansas.

A dust storm approaches Stratford, Texas, in 1935.

BLACK SUNDAY

Instead of a blizzard made of white snow, these *"Blizzards"* were made of dirt and dust so they were called *"Black Blizzards."* There were many severe black blizzards, but one of the worst of these events happened on April the 14th in the year 1935. The wind was traveling at a very high speed that day. Great dust walls formed in the atmosphere.

They were so big that they engulfed whole cities and blanketed regions. This particular dust storm was named *"Black Sunday."* The dust was so heavy and so thick that people couldn't see their own hands before their faces.

A farmer and his two sons during a dust storm in Cimarron County, Oklahoma, 1936, Photo: Arthur Rothstein.

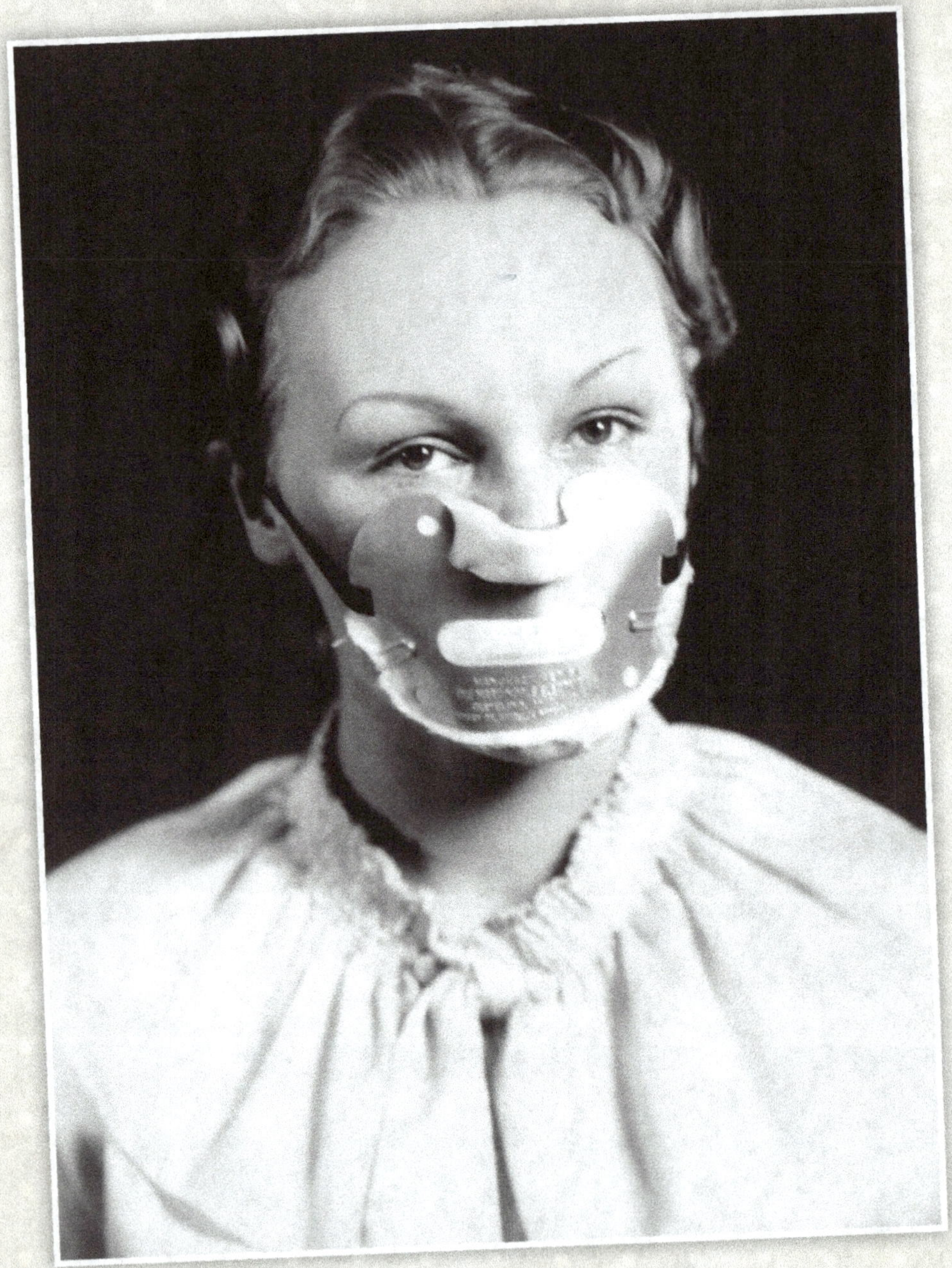

Dust mask developed for workers 1935.

It's hard to imagine how terrifying black blizzards truly were. Beginning in 1932, there were 14 such storms and they continued to increase in numbers almost every year with a peak of 72 storms in 1936. Millions of tons of dirt, soil, and dust swept off the bare, desert-like fields and twirled in the air. The dust had a terrible odor and was traveling at speeds up to 60 mph. If you were unfortunate enough to be outdoors with no shelter, the dirt would sting your face and choke you.

These terrifying events sometimes lasted over 10 hours with total blackout for most of that time. A single storm continued for up to 3 ½ days as the towering black column of dust reached a height of over 1000 feet from the ground.

*Huge boiling masses of dust that blocked
out the sun were common sights in Texas during
the Dust Bowl years.*

Some people feared that the world was coming to an end. Thousands of birds tried to escape the clouds but died from exhaustion as they tried to fly out. Wildlife that had no cover or burrow to duck into died on the ground from suffocation. Even indoors, if food was prepared, it had to be eaten immediately before a layer of dust and dirt settled on top of it.

Living during this siege of dust became almost impossible. Dust got into everything. It was very difficult to keep their dwellings free of the ever-present clouds of dust. They spent a lot of time trying to keep it out of their houses, but it was a losing battle. Even more severe of a problem was the fact that crops couldn't grow while the dust storms were happening.

Severely eroded farmland during the Dust Bowl,
circa 1930's

Their livestock was choking to death because of the dust. But the most severe problem of all was the loss of human life. Very few people had masks to protect them and just used wet cloths over their noses and mouths.

Farmer stands in a dust storm in New Mexico, Spring 1935.

The prolonged exposure to dust in their homes, clothing, food, and water had devastating consequences. Many people contracted a form of pneumonia caused by the dust and died when their lungs weakened. Babies, children, and elderly people were the most vulnerable because of their weaker lungs.

Farmer cultivating cotton on a farm during the Dust Bowl circa 1930's.

WHO WERE THE OKIES?

Now that there was no way to grow crops, many of the farmers of the Great Plains left for California thinking that there might be jobs there. Due to the economic hardships of the Great Depression, there were few jobs to be had. These farmers were desperate and they were willing to take any jobs and work hard for long hours.

Dorothea Lange's 1937 photo of a Missouri migrant family's jalopy stuck near Tracy, California.

If they didn't find work, their families would starve. The Californians called them *"Okies,"* which was a nickname for people who came from the state of Oklahoma. Over time, this term was used for any impoverished person or migrant farm worker who had come to California seeking work.

Florence Owens Thompson seen in the photo Destitute Pea Pickers in California. Mother of Seven Children. by Dorothea Lange

During the Dust Bowl, over three million people abandoned their farms and half a million went to other states. More than 6,000 people died just trying to hop on freight trains to travel out of the area.

Harvesting carrots in El Centro California Many
Dust Bowl drought refugees found jobs as farm
workers in California.

AID PROGRAMS

The U.S. Government started some programs to help the farmers that had remained on their lands. They began by teaching them advanced farming practices to help them nurture and preserve the soil. The government also purchased some of the region from the farmers and gave it time to regenerate so that future dust storms wouldn't happen. By the 1940s, much of the land in the Great Plains area had recovered from the *"Black Blizzards."*

North Dakota farmers waiting for their grants in a Resettlement Administration Office, 1936.

Photo shows two people walking along road towards Los Angeles, CA.

- People in California weren't happy about the influx of migrant workers into their state. In fact, they became fearful and paranoid about these desperate farmers. They passed a law that made it illegal for someone to bring poor people across the state lines. They established a border patrol called the *"Bum Blockade"* to keep the migrants out.

- About 60% of the people who were living in the Dust Bowl areas left their farms and traveled to other states to find work.

Dust storm, Elkhart, Kansas, May 1937.

- Finally, the rain arrived at the end of the 1930s and began to nurse the parched lands back to health.

- During the heavy periods of dust storms, farmers would hang clotheslines from their houses to their barns so that when they were outdoors they could find their way back home.

- The federal government planted a total of 220 million trees from Canada in the north to Texas in the south to provide a windbreak. This action was taken to help preserve the soil from blowing away in the wind.

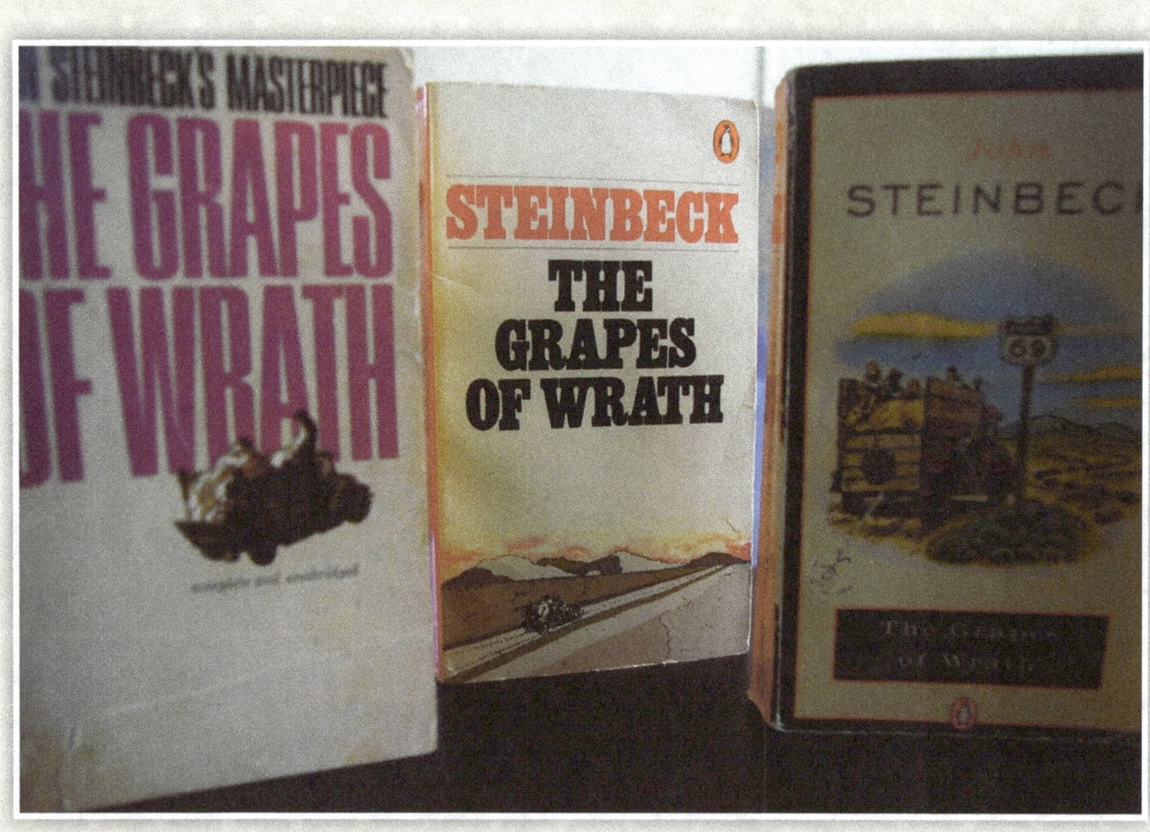
STEINBECK'S MASTERPIECE
THE GRAPES
OF WRATH
STEINBECK
THE
GRAPES
OF WRATH
66
STEINBECK

- The famous novel by John Steinbeck called *The Grapes of Wrath* is about a family living through the era of the Dust Bowl.

- It's believed that the term *"Dust Bowl"* was coined when the Associated Press ran an article by journalist Robert Geiger. He had been trapped in a black blizzard with his colleague, Harry Eisenhand, a photographer.

A migrant farm family in California, March 1935. Photo by Dorothea Lange.

19 CALIFORNIA 34
6C 12 99

Awesome! Now you know more about the Dust Bowl. You can find more Environment books from Baby Professor by searching the website of your favorite book retailer.

Farmer working his field after the Dust Bowl drought era.

Visit
BABY PROFESSOR
EDUCATION KIDS
www.BabyProfessorBooks.com
to download Free Baby Professor eBooks
and view our catalog of new and exciting
Children's Books